*The Girl in the Yellow Raincoat*

# The Girl in the Yellow Raincoat

*poems by*

## Anthony S. Abbott

St. Andrews College Press
Laurinburg, North Carolina

# Acknowledgments

*New England Review* for "After"

*Southern Poetry Review* for "Fool's Paradise," "Daisies," "Up the Rabbit Hole," and "Echoes of This Place"

*Cedar Rock* for "Geriatrics" and "Poem for Ruth"

*Crucible* for "Waves," "Leavings," "The Poet's Visit," "Shore Birds," and "Frost in August"

*St. Andrews Review* for "The Long Field" and "Walter Mitty Goes to New York"

*Anglican Theological Review* for "Seekers," "Not Wisely But Too Well," and "This Day"

*Cairn* for "Your Poem"

*Tar River Poetry* for "Blood Talk"

*Laurel Review* for "Incarnation," "Out of Mourning," and "Holy Family"

Davidson *Miscellany* for "Secrets"

*Cold Mountain Review* for "Long Distances"

*Lyricist* for "Morning Dreams," "Artist's Lives," "Covering the Dead," "Taking Care," "When You Came Back," "White Water," "Once Upon A Time," "Good Friday," and "The Man Who Had Lost Something"

*North Carolina Poetry Society Award Winning Poems* for "The Girl in the Yellow Raincoat," "Mary's Dream," "Poem for Robert Bly," and "First Love"

*Pembroke Magazine* for "Evening Light"

*Christianity and Literature* for "Out of that Darkness"

*Arts Journal* for "Letter to S."

*Kent Quarterly* for "Class Reunion" and "The New Magi"

*Carolina Literary Companion* for "Emergency Repairs," "Yesterday, My Father," and "Holding the Dark"

St. Andrews College Press
1700 Dogwood Mile
Laurinburg, NC 28352

Typeset in Palatino

Second Printing: January 1998

Third Printing: August 2002

*To Emily Abbott Nordfeldt
with love and gratitude*

# Contents

## The Girl in the Yellow Raincoat

## Fool's Paradise

# Once Upon A Time

# Up the Rabbit Hole

# The Girl in the
# Yellow Raincoat

# The Girl in the Yellow Raincoat

waits on the sidewalk outside
my window. The flower in her hair
is wet. She stands very still

her eyes focussed upward on some
object I cannot see. She does not
move, but she smiles . . . slightly.

Perhaps she plays the cello
and she is humming Bartók silently
making the bow ripple with her tongue

against her teeth. Or, maybe, she waits
for a bus to take her to her lover.
Or she has read a letter from Paris

or Istanbul and she smells coffee
and chestnuts steam roasted and she
hears in the cobbled streets the cries

of vendors under the aged curves
of bridges. Perhaps she is just a girl
standing in the rain by a stone bench

in the early morning while the
street shines. It is nothing—you argue.
Then why do I weep, and why are there

splinters in my palms, and why do I
stand here, long, long, after she is
gone?

# First Love

In the summer of my sixteenth year I ached
with love for a honey blonde from Phillips
Mill. Knowing nothing of how hands move
over a girl's skin, I only sat on the grass
as she fed chicken legs to a burly end
from New Hope High. Later, when he buzzed
down the road in search of beer, she touched
her lips to mine and placed her hand
on the inside of my thigh. My hands hovered
like whirlybirds above her back. My face played setting
sun to the coming night.

She laughed, told me I was cute, and drove
me home, spinning her tires in my gravel
drive. I tripped, backwards, up my kitchen
steps, spun like Nureyev to bed, and dreamed
the way boys dream.

Morning came, I worked in my neighbor's yard,
chopping vines and carrying them away.
For weeks, my fingers touched—nothing.

Once, white-gloved, I passed her on the street,
holding up my hand to give a sign. She walked on
blankly—like Ophelia trailing daisies down
the stone stairs to the river. Her face was
bruised.

I have not seen her since, but sometimes
in summer when the itch comes I dream of her
the way boys dream.

# Waves

As a child, I loved them, wading through
the stinging spray, head bent, eyes closed
against the salt, butting the sharp thrust
or ducking under, waiting for the moment,
catching, planing toward shore, breathing
once, then hold and down into the white
undertow, face, hands, ground by whirling
sand, then up and out, lungs bursting
onto the soft white beach.

Today a shark swirls in the shallows
while my son, on a sand bar farther out,
awaits the shoreward roll. "Wait," I scream
from the beach, but he has seen his wave
and skims, head down, toward the dark fin.

He rises smiling, eyes closed, palms gritty.
I rush to hug him, scanning the white foam
for the retreating fin. "Shark," I say.
He laughs and runs to the house for bait
and fishing line.

Later he's in again, stroking for the dark
water, then tumbling landward on the wave's curl.
Along the shore birds skitter for safety.

# White Water

Finally an act not of body but of mind
the body suffering learning to teach
the mind that the running of the river
is nothing more than a metaphor, and the

orange pumpkin helmets to keep
the brain from bursting on the savage
rocks and the thick soled sneakers are
only cushions for the mind's dream

which, with you or without you, I
will live, and if the helmet breaks
the brain pops like a cut melon,
but the pain is sweet as the raft

flies like a balloon down the chute,
bending, flipping its passengers gaily
into the chopping water, blithely
sailing on alone as the whirl sucks

us downward into the dark white and we
bounce with our sneakers as the guide
taught us, popping our heads to the top,
looking for help.

"Swim for the side,"
shouts the salesman with the purple hat
from the next raft, but I drive down
the middle still soaring with fear

as he reaches his arms, spider-like,
to me, dragging, pulling his catch
over the bulbous side, while my gills
gasp for air. Later we drink beer

and toss the cans in the slowing water.
It is late, the sky darkens and the rains
come. Too tired to strain, we watch
the thunder growl.

          The lightning poises
like a panther on the rocks above.
Pick me, I think. Now's a good time.
With you or without, I'm going down.

# Shore Birds

The shore birds march on the sea's
edge like commuters to the five
forty-five. Cheerful comedians
they bump and bob like ducks
in shooting galleries. Bandy-legged
clowns, they waddle forward
fluffing their fat bellies, darting
pencil beaks into the wet sand.
Pushed by higher waves, they merely
shift into overdrive.
        I follow close behind
my thoughts scarved and tangled. But
my feet trespass and they take wing
white feathers ringed by brown stabbing
the sky.
        Diamonds of the air, they are gone
into faster realms. I should joy in their
flight, scream for their grace on this gray
day. But I do not. Beloved clowns, I wish
you back, when I should wish you wings,
stumbler that I am.

# Poem for Ruth

You carry your soul in your hands, girl,
cupping it gently
like a bird's nest
with new blue eggs.

You show it to this person and that,
saying, "See how beautiful."
Your eyes sing
with the loveliness
of that soul.
It is one of the beautiful things
of this earth.

Once, at Christmas,
when you played "Silent Night"
on your violin to the green shirted
prisoners, you were mother,
daughter, sister with golden hair.
The darkness momentarily withdrew,
and even the hardest was touched.

But, beware, my friend.
Even then, beyond the fence
of that sainted moment
You were only a woman.

# Secrets

The green turtle swims shoreward
lays her eggs in the grainy sand
then scuttles for the sea's safety
before the shore birds can pluck
her heart out.
                    I watch this rhythm
from the second story of my beach house.
I have learned not to interfere.
I speak little. To say too much
is to lose everything.

# Morning Dreams

His life was patterns—dark winter
waiting, piercing glance of April,
slow gait of July, new mown hay
in August—crook-necked cows
in the meadow, pigs in the pock-
marked mud, thick-necked horses
neighing in the sloped barn.

In the world beyond, he thought,
were weasels and ocelots, fire
in the night, jagged glass on
tenement floors, slashes, smells,
and men with scars who vanished
and were found months later stuffed
in lock boxes in foreign airports.

I could have told him of the wave's curl
and the sun's flash on tall glass,
I could have said, "Look" and kissed
him, but I didn't. I only left
him standing there, flat footed
in the blue innocence of his
morning dreams.

# Poem for Robert Bly

You swirl before me, Robert, a golden
lamp. I rub you for truth and you burn.
You dance, robed and masked, to the sound
of dulcimer. You resuscitate the mysteries.

I came, like others that day, to muse on sky
and earth and the fine shapes of leaves
hidden under water. I, too, made lines
from sounds and shapes and colors. I too

made *haiku*. O God, I hear your laughter now.
Poems are not made from scanned exercises
of the mind. They are stains in dark graves,
knives in flesh, white stones on gravel roads.

I did not come that day to write, I came
for you, Robert, and dreamed that you might
pull me from the sad shelves of memory
from the dock of forgotten desire into the sweet

mystery of the mother. My wife laughs at you,
Robert, and says my knees look funny. I cannot
make the lotus position. But I have heard
the scorched belly of your words, and I know

you wait for me in the eye of the fire.

# Your Poem

would be small
like the Japanese maple

soft like green moss
beside streams

delicate as
the wren's neck.

It would smell
of jasmine.

If you touched it
feathers would fold

under fingers
and it would cry

silently as ice
and sing

like the nightingale
in dark forests.

Its words would look
upward at the stars

dance dizzily
down the page

and tired, slide sideways
into sleep.

# Frost in August

The days are all thumbs
gray black clouds humping rain
into the already sodden earth.
Mushrooms and strange weeds proliferate
in uncut yards.

The river is dark and high
docks soft algae ridden
muddy pawprints of dogs on floors
children crying
mothers and lovers of the sun
snapping waspish

And still you shine through this.
I think of spring when blossoms come—
forsythia, jonquils, dogwood—
early blossoms and frost
pure crystals whiting the lawn.

It covers us
holds us preserved with some new sight
so brief and fine
that late risers laugh
and wink at wild imagination.

You know enough of day
and what it does.
I think that you are frost
coming in the night and going
so soon.

# Class Reunion

It has rained all day, grey upon grey.
I stare west at some imagined spot
of blue. I pace the room, circle
the table like an old dog, then sit,

returning to the faces of the past,
those curiously clean open faces,
wrenlike, white as the shoes we wore
to graduate, kneeling on the chapel

floor, dovesin a line, feeling
the headmaster's hand blessing our
unruly heads. We marched into the sun
of June better than our elders, icy men

in black silk socks and wing tip shoes
whose women glided silently from room
to room in shawls and woolen dresses.
They were granite and gin, florid of face

cynical as ground glass. We did not know
the rain then. Now we are fifty and come
once more to kneel on the cold stone
of the chapel floor. We will bring

our grey for blessing and find the faces
of the boys we were shining underneath.

# The Man Who Had Lost Something

stood by the side of the road
looking down at the gravel shoulder
where milkweed tried to grow.

He remembered the poem by James Wright
about the horses, but there were
no horses to bless him.

He remembered the woman whose fingers
were smaller than the rain,
but he knew no such woman himself.

He thought he might like to die
for some great cause, but there was
no cause he cared for.

He wished to be kind, he wished
to be fair, to be just
to be unselfish

but these things did not help him
find the object for which he was
searching.

There was a button, to be sure,
a shining chip of mica, a wisp
of cellophane, a discarded piece

of Wrigley's Spearmint gum, a graphite
pencil and a notebook paper with "Marcia"
scrawled in green pen near the corner.

He had loved once, this man,
and the pain was like a red scar
which had burst into a shower

of sparks—green and vermillion.
And he cried out—"Never Again!"
Then he was quiet for a long, long time.

Until one day he knew he must
look along the side of the road
among the juniper and tar

for the thing which he had lost.

# Fool's Paradise

# Fool's Paradise

In my town it is dark by eleven.
Blue Fords sleep in grey garages
and the leaves are piled on curbs
in neat green bags. Muggers and
rapists pine from lack of work.
Even the dogs are silent, curled
in flealess dreams on thick shag rugs.

I dream of something different
like Halloween costumes at Sunday
tea, pumpkins on church steeples
and sheep painted Richard Petty blue
quietly eating the village green.

My parents never saw the sunrise sober.
They danced in fountains, trailing
the idols of the age from bar to bar
'till the liquor turned their minds
and my mother's fingers stiffened
on the keys and the notes echoed
sourly in the yellow dawn of Walfare
Island where they took her stomach out
and left her to die screaming
in the crowded halls. The hospital's
just a memory now, an item mentioned
on the Circle Line tour by guides
who say the price of condominiums
is high owing to the view.

In my town the people rise early
and the sun screams off the sugar
maples in the early fall. My sisters,
loosed from the dark arms of the cities
where they live, call it paradise.
I only tuck my tail under my doctor's
gown and grin. "For fools," I say.

# Blood Talk

This one wades in thick hip boots,
grey green slick in the deep water,
purple fly pinned to the pocket
of the red flannel shirt. Flip of
the wrist and the line spins outward

. . . another spins yarns, crouched
on his wet thighs in the red shadow
of a Tennessee barn, spitting tobacco,
easy in the twilight air. Horses,
cows, pigs rut in the background.

And me? With no fisherman father,
no thicklipped mountain grandad,
no maiden aunt, starving, lace collared,
in the root cellar of her ante-bellum
home, no spittle drooling, Bourbon

drinking, twang talking uncles,
no chickens scratching in the yard,
no fast sweating mares, no garden,
my God, not even tomatoes or radishes,
or cross cut saw to cut winter wood.

I got nothing but goddam words working
for me, and everyone knows that words
aren't real, aren't flesh and blood,
and country-Southern like Bibles
and Red Man, and dreams, and blood.

# Artist's Lives

### 1

There are mornings in between when the autumn
leaves still green but yellow edged stir
under the breeze's cap, and the honey colored
sun warms the windows and the woman slips
to sleep in the brown chair by the easel.
The brush drops to the splattered floor
and the calico cat jumps, then chases the ball
under the sofa where the long dog sits.

The woman dreams of frosted ponies in the crisp
air of Minnesota, of skates sliding on the thick
ice, of bells and sleds and scarves and hatted
children screaming joy through steamy mouths.

She wakes, puzzled by the warmth, then shakes
her fingers, coaxing the blood, mixing the paints.
There is ice in her eyes, and on the canvas ice
appears, whitish grey with fish beneath, green
and black with red eyes, and quick blue arcs
in the sky.

### 2

The sun dips to the southwest. It will be cold
by five. The woman sets her easel by the pond's
edge. On the far side in a yellow field the dog
chases a monarch butterfly. On a lily pad a green
frog courts a fly. From under a hawthorn bush
the calico cat watches the frog. The woman waits.

The frog is green marble, motionless, lidded,
dormant as petrified wood. The fly forgets,

then the tongue lashes, quick as a mosquito's
eye. In the field the dog leaps at the butterfly,
tail curled, head pointed, feet off the ground.
The dog's soul is weightless as eternity.

The woman paints the frog's tongue and the dog's
soul with the cat watching.

3

Night now, and the woman lies in bed
while willow branches scratch at her window.
Calico warms her feet. The long dog touches
her side. She dreams of seas and black Pacific
rocks, of cliffs and caves and the clacking
horns of mountain rams, of jade and opal
and silver in the earth.

4

In the grey morning she wakes early. Wrens
beg by the feeder. The cat mews, the dog
stretches and cries. The letters on the desk
open their mouths for food. Death rides
the tractor in the far field, cutting the hay.
By ten he's done. He knocks, but she's gone,
down the dirt road, easel in hand, to the brook
to see how light falls on stones under moving
water. He picks his teeth awhile, then drives
away in a black '57 Chevrolet. From the corner
of her eye she catches him and laughs. No time
for him today.

24

# Transfiguration

Over my daughter's head
gold leaves thrust skyward into blue.
She is all light.
She is fire and air.
She rises, slowly, haloed—
diffusing into the stuff of leaf itself.

I am all tree,
I am bark and branch,
I stumble, rooted, held
by the humpness of limbs.
Our elements will not mingle.

Come down, love,
come down
and color me gold before you go.

# Not Wisely But Too Well

The walls of my study are white, the door
and the shelves white. When the blinds
are pulled, even the windows are white.

If I sit a long time without speaking
I begin to believe that God will walk
in the door like cream rising to the top.

The other day I went to see my son
play soccer. He's tall with a summer
tan and sad soft eyes the girls like.

My heart pounds crazily for him. Up
and down the field he runs, then—crack!
He falls, Hector below the walls of Troy.

I swallow my heart and pray. Across the way
I see the other team—laughing. "You dirty
bastards!" I scream. My eyes blur. I run

toward them. "You're sick," I hiss into
their coach's ear. Blue shirted Trojans
circle my fallen son. I cannot look.

I sit in my white study and gaze
at the white walls. I wait for God
to enter. I watch . . . for signs.

# When You Came Back

I thought of Pound's "In a Station of the Metro"
and the way your mind leaps, arriving before
the others have left the house. I thought of

thick black coffee at stained tables and the
firmness of your stride, the courage you carry
as simply as the center of your father's heart.

I thought of women with long braided hair
and bearded men waggling fingers at the darkness
there where you can palm it through the wet stones.

When you came back I thought of the *troisieme etage*
of Hotel Excelsior and the maid's face when she brought
croissants and jam to my bed early in the morning.

I rode the fast trains and spoke only French.
I wrote long letters full of scenery and hope
and big words about the spires of Gothic cathedrals.

I could have done something then, reached out
and touched the scars of our ineptitude. You carry
that baggage now, lightly and with large heart.

They will not help you much, these wood-sprite children.
They think the darkness is a lie, and the knife in the
heart an image from the folded pages of old books.

The other day, in the yard, my friend, playing ball
with his young son, paused and said, "We haven't
suffered enough." We meaning all of us, we meaning

the woodsprites, those berries on the path to be
eaten by the birds. But not you. Not you.
You are wheat. You are rain. You make us live again.

# Distances

I had only wanted to talk to you
to take my rage at distances
and hurl it somewhere

missing your smile and the way
you cock your head
pretending to be angry
knowing what I will say
before I have finished thinking it.

I see the great layered rocks
thrust up from the past
and the river below
in no hurry but its own
as the car with its sleeping passengers
speeds by on the lined road.

Center of my winding self,
guardian of my journeys,
stand by me in the slow rain
and the drifting mountain mists,
watch over me in the coming dark.

# Evening Light

The trees undress slowly from the top.
Bare arms arc brownly into the sky. It is
sunset. Orange skirts swirl in an awful
dying light. The ground is littered gold.

I stop the scene with the shutter of my eye—
stop and hold and mark—this blue, these reds
and holding greens—those rusts upon the ground.
I stoop and pick and hold this one dry leaf.

It crumbles in my hand, and I see a picture
from the morning paper speak as if alive.
Five Turkish children killed by earthquake
lie upon the ground, seemingly asleep.

The mother screams above, mouth horror ravaged,
while in Kentucky and Ohio other mothers weep
into clean white handkerchiefs as taps are played
and flags are placed into their hollow laps.

Hats do not suffice. The time is never right.
Beauty is always almost gone. This dress, this
cock of the head, this touch, this curl of hair,
this greying beard, that look over the shoulder.

We are taken so suddenly, the breath goes
in white astonishment. If I had known is not
enough. Say it now. Say it now. Say it now.
Before the shutter clicks once more and closes.

# Out of Season

It is November, the air redolent,
thick with mulch. My son, unwillingly
drawn from Saturday dreams, pushes
the mower through the thickening leaves.
I stand on the high ladder, locking
storm windows into place.

But across the way tomatoes still ripen.
Below me, bushes smell like gardenias.
Dizzy, I close my eyes, pressing my face
against the clouding glass.

Then, wordlessly, I fall.

# Taking Care

Outside it is raining. My brown bicycle
turns slowly browner. Columns of water
march unimpeded through the Fiat's open
window onto the cracked vinyl seat. Things
cry out for care—leaves to be raked,
gutters cleared, wires spliced, hinges
oiled. In the bathroom, on den shelves,
down the dark hall, plants groan hoarsely
for spray. Mice in corners of closets
chuckle with delight. I am idle, amused
by the animation of things. I slouch
in the broken chair, its springs popping,

and think of you. "Take care," we say—
meaning what? Drive slowly? No smoking,
drinking? Careful meaning slow, careful
meaning don't let go? Careful meaning
holding tight to the reins—conscience
and brains and the tidy calculations
of the CPA? Economics 101A?

We know better, you and I, caretakers
that we are. "Take care," we say, meaning
*cara*, dear, meaning full of preciousness,
meaning we are gifts to one another
like those marble veined old women in print
dresses, those moppers of floors you see
stealing near dawn from buildings on lower
Broadway, stockings rolled below their knees,
necks crimped stiff from twisted work.

On checkered floors they keep the blacks
black and the whites white. We keep the light
in one another's eyes with apples, jokes and charms.

Go well, friend. May you have scarves on snowy
afternoons and water under docks in June. Mount
slowly. Breathe easy. And ride.

# Incarnation

Forget the virgin birth, the stable,
the cattle lowing and all that.
Maybe Mark was right . . . he just
arrives. John, waist deep in water,
sees him first, striding toward Jordan,
hands bleeding, heels blistered
from walking barefoot down
the muddy ruts of roads.

He had never seen pain before. Never
watched a man die. In a thicket
one day he saw a fawn chew
its leg off to escape a trap.
Later he passed a corpse hanging
from a cross along the road.
So this is what it's like,
he thought. They'd never taught him
about pain up there.

So, he thinks, washing the dust off
in the river, feeling the touch
of John's hand upon his head,
this is what it means to be human.

# Geriatrics

From the white sanctuary
of the nurse's station
I look down the long green
Corridors. Men from the right,
Women from the left.

They will come soon
with that slow shuffling walk,
some on crutches, some with canes,
slippers scraping, sliding
along the smooth floor.

Worst are the wheelchairs rolling
steadily down the echoing halls.

My starched white uniform
is too short, too thin
to hide me from their marble
gaze. Some night I think
that I will scream to see them,

eyes cold, spittle drooling
from their lips, hands out
begging to kill the pain
for one more night and send them

into dreams of times when limbs
were whole and skin was soft
and eyes could see.

# Long Distances

He talks on the phone without
his teeth. I can't make out
the words. He says he'd write
but the arthritis has swollen

his fingers. Sometimes he dictates
to his sister, who's crippled
with a cracked ankle. Her guru's
in jail in India. They're

raising money for his release.
The brother drives to town for
groceries and the mail. She curses
him. "You steal my checks," she says.

He locks himself in the room upstairs
and sets the stereo on automatic.
He only steals the cash. Checks are
made out to GURU RELEASE FUND.

He cuts the grass, repairs the screens,
shovels the walks in winter, and tells
her she's a sucker. She writes me
that she can't stand it much longer.

# Once Upon A Time

# Holding The Dark

The day is dark
        like rivers in December
                like leaves buried under sand.

Inside the brightly lighted room
        mouths flutter like butterflies
                to keep away the blackness.

I stand alone outside
        holding the dark in my hands
                like a gift from another land.

I think the dark is our child
        born of the moon on winter nights
                and silence after kissing.

Once we took her to the woods
        to lose her like Gretel in the tale.
                She followed the white stones home.

Now she curls herself between us
        touching our lips and eyes
                with her white fingers.

She takes our words and turns them
        to slow notes on blues pianos
                to songs heard before first light.

She whispers in our ears during sleep
        and we wake in her strange starshine
                more tightly wed.

# Mary's Dream

*"Did she put on his knowledge with his power. . . ?"*
                              —*William Butler Yeats*

Jesus at the lathe in the afternoon sun,
hairs blonding on the brown arms, nick
on the finger from some mishap
                              she at the window
frames the moment before the crazy
honeycombed John with his damned prophecy
comes upsetting Herod, starting heads rolling
and the sneer of the scribes unravelling
her son's life.
                              Who was Joseph anyway
to get her in this mess with his stupid
lineage?
                              And did she not dream, scream
nightly the hours on the cross, nails
in her own palms, waking at dawn, looking
across at his sleeping face and for an instant
so scared her breath stopped
                              being mother first
and God second    her son dying    why not someone
else's    what had she done anyway
                              blunt edged Joseph
would never understand the lake of glass
where they would stop and be left alone.

# The Long Field

All night the snow falling fine
white flakes. By morning the long
field's as fresh as your dreams.

In the paper yesterday I read
of two teenaged boys who killed
their father. "He was mean,"
they said . . . "Never let us do nothin'."
So they shot him in the leg
and the shoulder and once more
in the back of the head as he tried
to run out the door. Afterwards
they bought junk food and electric
games and new clothes with his VISA card.

Outside my steps are the first marks
of the morning. I walk for both
of us, remembering your words:

"From the house to the woods
is about three hundred yards.
The long field in between's
your life. Walk it every day
from end to end and mind what the seasons tell you.
The rain in your face won't hurt you
or the snow in your boots.
Keep one eye on the brass weathervane
and the other on the sun."

The father, it seems, walked his boys
to school each day. And when he left
for work they turned around and went home.

# Letter to S.

Cold here. In front of the
post office the sidewalk buckles.
The campus dogs lie in each others'
laps for warmth.
Your horse is out to pasture
wearing his winter woolies.
The girl who used to ride him
has gone south
(pregnant, the women say,
chattering at their mailboxes).
They've taken axes to your oak,
selling it by the cord for firewood.

Cathy's in Berkeley, living with Steve,
Claire's quit school,
Jana leaves for Texas in two weeks
and since the plumbing leaks
I've boarded up the house
and moved my stuff to Susie's until spring.
We've got a bird with a hurt wing
we feed sunflower seeds to.
Otherwise we don't do much
but talk of you.

We walked to town today
kicking stones along the way
down the frozen dirt road
thinking of the night last May
we walked home drunk and barefoot
and wiped the blood off in the bath.

The times are bad. I get letters
from Oral Roberts who says a nine
hundred foot Jesus wants my dimes.

The Baptists in the country north
of us have banned *Brave New World*.
Shetland sweaters proliferate
like rabbits.

Don't come back.

They look at me like my hair's dirty.
I never knew cold before.

# Halfway Covenant

Cold now. Sky like the silence
of ice. Snow muffles the sound
of my feet. The Soviets are marching
on Tehran, and the Christian judge
next door proclaims the world
will end in August, 1984.

If it does we'll have to meet
halfway the day before—setting
off with a change of underclothes
leaving socks unsorted, peanut
butter sticking to the kitchen sink,
kids at the pool, spouses stuck
in some gigantic traffic jam.

Motels will be sold out.

# Seekers

The angel had said to follow
the star, but not believing
in angels, nor seeing any star
we could distinguish from the
others we had known before, we
only stood puzzled, looking at
one another like passengers whose
bus has suddenly and inextricably
broken down on a dark country road.

So we would have to begin again
learning where to look and how
to look, learning to peek under
the corners of carpets and behind
winks, and around the tears of
children, and the grey stares of
old men, learning to squint past
the edges of the sun in the early
morning and under its pink folds
at night, learning again to take
one step at a time toward the
wonder, listening for the lost sounds
of ducks swimming in the silk mist
of silent December lakes,

watching for the Christ child behind
untimely births and early deaths,
over and above the dark stain of our
clumsy laws and mumbled words, not
merely waiting for the act which
after all has been enacted once for
all and is ever being enacted
but watching and learning to follow
its signs, to read the map to that
obscure country where the senses will
smell God and hear Him in the undiscovered
sounds that stay after the horns have
ceased and the dust has cleared.

# Holy Family

In the rubble of small villages east
of Naples bulldozers grunt down once
streets in the silence of night. No one
wishes to watch. No one wishes to see
human arms and legs sifted in the yellow
mouths.

White masked soldiers look for the
living, but the work is slow,
and there are no volunteers, only newsmen
from America circling in white helicopters,
only onlookers with moonlike eyes standing
at safe distances, only children walking
the lines of the dead lifting blankets,
only young men searching the wards of makeshift
hospitals for eyes under the white bandages.

"Benvenuti a Sant' Agnelo dei Lombardi"
says the sign at the town's entrance,
but the mayor is dead and the aldermen
are missing, and still on the third day
there are no volunteers.
                              "Why?" they ask.
The earth shakes again the the Pope walks
among them, placing his hand on the heads
of the wounded and the dead. He is all
in white, white in the dust of the dead
and the cries of those who still live
in their fifth day under the earth.

Is it our sin, father?" a young man asks,
holding his hat in both hands.

"Who cares?" grumbles the officer, his face
caked with mud. "We need volunteers," he hisses,
"and they send us a Pope. Publicity," he mutters
angrily, and kisses the old man's hand.
Stubborn and straight old man, dressed in white,
bitter remnant of worlds on worlds grown obsolete
in the ripeness of time, you carry the stench
of death. But the old man knows. He makes
the sign of the cross, and the bulldozers stop,
the soldiers stop, and the young men mourning
their wives and children stop.
                          "No," he answers,
"but God never said we wouldn't die." His face
is neither kind nor sad, it simply carries God.
That is all. *Emmanuel.* God with us. That is all.
On the seventh day it snows.

# Out of that Darkness

1

The stable is always somewhere else.
The hooked noses of the old astrologers
and the stains on their robes remind us
that the camels they rode must have smelled
of dung and the child they saw there was
not at all what anyone wanted.
How cold was Mary?
Did Joseph wonder?

2

We cling to the comfort of known griefs—
broken arm at twelve, the bicycle run over
in the driveway, Aunt Abigail's fussiness,
Uncle Peter's asthma, the yellow melancholy
of grandfather George—but not that darkness
out there.
Snow in the field. The dog's footprints
stop at the edge of the paved road.

3

Even then he was strange
child in the temple
Simeon's prayer granted    he would pierce
his mother's heart    woman what have I to do
with thee. Yes, trampling the robes of the Pharisees
this man singing off key. He never would make
cantor or elder either. His feet dirty, his thoughts
on the guts of the poor and children's eyes.

4

We are harder to find. City, suburb, town,
village, country. Houses thin. Outside white.
Inside the fire mesmerizes. Frost on the window
holds all in outer space.
                    Over the field Christ walks
toward us, galoshes unbuckled
                    and green scarf torn.

# The New Magi

It is dusk. The sun has tipped backward
behind the old town hall. Inside the patterned
windows of the church, candles nod to candles
until it seems the world is only light
and festive voices singing "Silent Night."

Out of the dark the siren wails, once,
twice, a third time, and grinding gears
disturb the "all is bright," while somewhere
in another town a black man in a stocking cap
folds quilts around himself to stop the night.

Out of the dark the siren wails and somewhere
in another town a woman flushes yesterday's news
from under the rest room door and a red haired
girl with shrouded eyes holds out her hand
to strangers walking through the station's

swinging doors. Where is the star that calls you,
black man? Where is the star that seeks you,
woman? Where is the star that lifts you, shrouded
girl? Walk to us, now, over the battered highways.
Walk to us slowly over the rutted roads.

Walk to the siren's wail, and the grunting sound
of fire in the night. Throw open the church's door.
Walk with your papers and your quilts and the sorrow
in your eyes, bringing your gifts past the carpet
of our candles to the manger's straw. Kneel and turn

And bid us follow with our light up the long aisle
out, out into the grace of the beckoning night.

# Eye of a Needle

The rich live in quilted souls.
They are soft like the spaces between bones

in children. They smell of musk and otter.
They muffle the rattle of our broken drums

with the cottoned distances of green lawns
and the grey stone of gateways.

They circle above us like strange birds
from the islands of the south. They rise

like Pharoh from chairs of state
and we defer to the black pearl of rank.

We ape their ways, looking upward
from bellies, half in hatred, half in love.

Save us from such dreams, Lord. Teach us
to lie low, to take rain in the face,

to feel the seasons full and nurse
from humility's spoon. Then may we

at the knocking hour crawl patiently
raw-kneed and naked to the stable door.

# From Another Angle

The blessed dead rest in our hearts
like the tunes of youth. Their melodies
mingle with the stuff of now. Their faces
mix in our dreams with images of Christmas.

Mary all in blue cradles my daughter
in the crescent of her arms. My father
stands behind like Joseph—quilted,
turbaned, puzzled by the strange brightness.

A cry of camels and the streets shine
gold. My mother trailing white brings
frankincense. Aunts and uncles long since
passed march forward with the mystery of myrrh.

Gabriel in the guise of my fairy godmother
carries the star through back streets of our town
calling us all to Bethlehem. We stumble
from our dark doors into the madness of light.

We cry the moment of our new birth. We walk
hand in hand with shepherds from the hills
of Kentucky. Everywhere, from Carolina
to the mountains of the West there is music.

# Once Upon A Time

There were wise men once.
We search for their bones now
and the places where they walked
have become shrines.

We stand quietly, baring our heads
and mark the names inwardly.
We commit to memory words that they have spoken.
We chip pieces of their stones
and carry them in our pockets as talismans.

We hope for truth beyond the numbered pieces
of our days, and we turn to the old story.
"Once upon a time" we say, there were wise men
and shepherds who came to see the child
born of Mary.

The unnamed sculptor holds the mystery of his stone,
as the child fully formed
stands in his mother's womb.
He speaks
and the stone carries his silent words.
We wait his wisdom. We carry the strength
from the stone to our wandering hearts.

Then the green typhoon of Reformation.
Black gowned Calvinists batter images of God
and the saints to broken dust.
Shrines once filled with pilgrims
grow only ivy over ruined stone.
Later, in a calmer time, these walls become
houses and apartments where people dwell
invoking the spirit of the past for protection.

The sculptor's work emerges, hidden for centuries,
under the church floor.
Men stand in line and marvel at its workmanship.
They gaze at its figures
and believe nothing.

Famine stalks the land.
Children with swollen bellies and seared
lids raise their hands for help.
Muscular men chew their flesh
and litter the roads
with their small bones.

We turn and turn
arriving in the dust of our own track.

Once upon a time
a child was born
and wise men came
there were wise men once
upon a time.

# Daisies

It snowed last night.
On the hill behind the church
my boots make the first prints
of the morning.

With my mittened hand
I scrape the snow from your marker.

I talk.
I wait and then
walk home

watching the grey birds circle the steeple
watching the tram car lines
watching the steam in windows.

I look down. The street is littered
with daisies.
I carry them, sleeping, to my house.
I set them on the kitchen table.
They glow like gold crowns.

The room swells, while outside
the snow darkens the windows.

# Leavings
*(for my father)*


Outside my window a gnarled old oak
leans precariously on his elbow
snarling at his successors
wrapped smugly in their canvas diapers
and waiting
                  to be lowered
into the hard winter earth.

The other arm is gone,
the socket painted closed
with that preservative we use
to keep the old from rotting.

Knots bulge from his side like tumors.

Still
        I think I like him better
than all those thin skinned babies
packed tightly
                in their little holes.

He's not so predictable.
In the spring he'll flower strangely
and dance his own configurations
in the wind.

Bless you, old brother.
May my leavings be so rich.

# Walter Mitty Goes to New York

Snow on the turnpike, patches of ice, busses,
trucks buzzing toward the funnel into the city—
a women, pale, alone, Buick perhaps, slips,
spins, now turned facing the oncoming dinosaurs, hands
before her face, eyes wide, terror beyond imagining

*and I leap from my car, dodging the Big Mack*
*pulse slighly elevated but astronautically calm,*
*speaking words of wisdom let it be lady, shielding*
*her from the . . .*

Later, in the subway, uptown express purple green
with graffiti a man black and bearded faded army
jacket sleeps on the seat. I balance tentatively . . .
train lurching forward . . . he rolls, mouth open,
eyes glass, warm puddle on the seat

                    *and I speak,*
*leaning, placing his arm over my shoulder, edging*
*him to stared shock of Saks shoppers toward*
*the door and up the stairs to the contagious*
*hospital where Jon Gannon waits with Kildare smile*
*send me the bill, I grin Quincylike . . .*

At the Philharmonic in Avery Fisher Hall
white buns buzz at the intermission. Talk
is indistinguisable from the soft roar of
jackhammers on a distant avenue. Scream!
A purse is gone, brown jacketed boy running
for the exit

*A quick dive and three karate chops, knee*
*on back, arm twisted tight, smiling James*
*Bond like, your purse Mrs. Rockefeller.*

During the Ravel I sleep soundly.

# Emergency Repairs

My godmother
a remarkable woman
drove racing cars
smoked Fatimas
and made love to my father
under my mother's nose.

Years later
when she told me
I told her also
of my loves.
"You don't hurt people"
was all she said
before she climbed
to her room and closed
the door.

Every morning I
look at this small leaf
pointed and flecked
in white
and in February
at the first forsythia.

Saturdays I bake
date nut bread for
the Shut ins
and cookies for the green
shirted prisoners.

I walk the dog at night
and do not step on any cracks.

My godmother has
a new aorta
made of nylon.
She travels to New Guinea.
She feels good
because all the fat
which was killing her
has been scraped away.

She is proud of me.

# Going Down

A man appears. He speaks to me.
He is a friend and I have forgotten
him and his wife and the name
of his child. As he talks, I listen

to the wind outside, blowing
through the cedar. I hear the beat
of my heart though the inner ear.
I see the hairs on his wrist

and the nicotine on his fingers.
His words crumple like waste paper.
He rises, extends his hand.
My fingers are cold.

# Up the Rabbit Hole

# Up the Rabbit Hole *or* Oz Remembered

1

Think of the whole thing in reverse—
Dorothy whirling back from Oz
onto the flat plains of Kansas saying
"Yes, Auntie Em, I do love you"
Think of Alice flying up the rabbit hole
onto the green English grass.

Think of winter's day
Alice before the mirror
Dorothy under the quilted spread
Winter is Kansas. Winter is England.

Back there it was MGM over the rainbow technicolor
It was smile in the trees and letters
under doors and brown bottles to make you grow

It was the twirl of a lion's tail
and witches wilting into water

2

We wait for the snow to melt. We wait
for the sun. We stumble into the unfamiliar
sound of birds and the slant light of spring.

Alice searches in the grass for the rabbit hole.
The wheat of Kansas stands endless.

We cannot find our way back, choose our way
back. We can only wait.

Does it hurt—this time between?
Like death—it hurts
like ice on the bone
like marrow scraped

but it is only the silence before . . .
the beginning.

# This Day

is cold and dark with the wind
like a bear snorting under ice,

is small and thin like a moth
with one wing falling,

is still like the silence
of night before first dawn,

hurts like a child crying
for its mother after fright,

is low and patient
like a white sheet over scars.

She stands under a bare
tree, its limbs chipped and marred.

She shows me the swollen bellied
cracked lipped children.

She snaps the branch of my
petty anger like God laughing:

"I am short and squat with crooked
teeth and my dress pulls tight

across the waist. My pock marked
skin ripples when I walk."

"Love me," her eyes say,
and again, "Love me,

for I am all your day.
Without me there is nothing."

I pale and know that she is right,
but still I stand, kicking sand

into the grey rain and waiting
for the wind to bring it back again.

Only the saints can choose
to love such days. Only the saints.

# Echoes of this Place

### 1

We have lived here too long, bricked in,
straight lines and trapezoids.
We speak with authority of leather bound books
we speak like bells.

### 2

I sit among my books in my white room.
I am silent. A woman enters.
"Something very bad has happened," she says.
She closes the door. A man, it seems, has hurt her,
someone she knew and liked, someone she respected.
She is angry—she sits straight and tells
her story without tears. She is angry
that this should happen here
where shapes are thin and fine like crystal.

### 3

I think suddenly of my mother dying
in a grey hospital on Welfare Island
her bed rolled into the hall
because they needed the room.
Where was I?
Courting some girl from Vassar
lisping scotch under the Biltmore Clock.

### 4

It is noon now. The woman has gone.
I like the clear eyed sharpness of her hate.
"He touched me where you do not touch," she said.

She will pay him back a thousandfold.
But we are soft.
We sit in our white spaces, watching.

5

Outside it is March, and branches beat on our windows.
Tin roofs tumble down back alleys.
Drivers are buried in shifting drifts of snow.
At my mother's funeral they rolled her casket in
through a side door I had not known was there.
Then they made me look at her painted face.
Here we close our caskets
and drape graves with spring flowers.

# The Poet's Visit

At the window of the college guest house
I sip coffee with the poet. She asks
the name of the bird that sings
outside. I cannot tell her.

You grow roses under your mother's
window and pour seeds in the feeder
for the white throated sparrow.

The poet sits in my office. My plant
coughs. I give it water. She asks
its name. I cannot tell her.

In your mother's house you bend
to water violets and hyacinths
which bloom once among the stones
and die. You pluck dead leaves
from the swaying philodendron.

The poet has read well. We walk home
slowly under the stars. She is tired.
She asks the name of the large yellow
star in the west. I do not know.

Outside your mother's house you watch
Jupiter and his four moons,
you offer prayers to the Pleiades,
the seven daughters of Atlas.

Alone I know only dirt and grasses
Tomorrow I will buy books and read.

# Yesterday, My Father

*In memory of Howard J. Abbott (1904-1982)*

### 1

Yesterday, my father, I sat upon your bed
holding your gnarled sticks of fingers.
I told you of my son, and your tears mixed
with mine over the spilled ribbons and paper.

Later we laughed and I played the clown,
as always. But you had forgotten your part.
Yours eyes gripped me fiercely, "I am dying,"
you said—a word we never used before.

Then the pain took you, hard under the heart,
and my breath went black and I remembered
the green laugh of the Wicked Witch of the West.
I left silently before the others came.

### 2

Today, my father, you sit upon my bed—
slim and white like the Prince of Wales
on a summer cruise—your fingers curled
'round the handles of two brown bags.

"Watcha got there, kid?" I ask, hunching.
"My pain" is what you say. "It's too
heavy. May I put it down?" You look once
and leave . . . before the others come.

My mind plays on in a thousand thousand
ways like a scarlet tanager grubbing
for worms in the April earth. I like
to think you will return.

# Covering the Dead

A soldier with a shovel scrapes away
the earth, and for the first time
the skin of the nuns shines white
against the sun. I think of the flesh
of my friend in prison and the way
his eyes have turned color.
                              I visit him.
We talk slowly under the deep green
oak, while the dogwoods flower beyond
the fence. His anger burns.
                              I tell him
of my drive to New York, of the woman
on the Pennsylvania Turnpike, her car
spinning on the ice, eyes wide, fingers
bloodless on the sterile wheel.
                              I tell him
of the old man asleep on the seat
on the Broadway local, warm trickle
of urine running down his leg.
                              I stand
and take my friend's hand. Parole
will come soon, I say. I walk through
the gate and drive home where I sit
in a darkened room and watch pictures
from El Salvador.
                              I walk into the garden.
I stroll among the rhododendron. I inhale
deeply. I sprinkle dirt lightly on the bodies,
then flowers.

# Good Friday

My son lounges before the television
his legs draped over the falling arm
of the chair, his eyes fixed on other
eyes, his lips tight. The story on

the screen is familiar. Jesus before
Pilate, but my son has never seen it—
not this way at least. Christ is sinewy,
lean, steel blue eyes piercing the flesh

of the soft politician. Pilate is easy.
He loves his wife, his wine, his silk sheets.
The fierce Sadduccees sicken him. He likes
Jesus, and I am drawn against my will

by the sudden nearness of the old tale.
My son and I are silent. We listen to the once
familiar words. Suddenly, voices in the hall
and lights from every side. Bags crinkle,

Heels click on the wooden floor. My wife
is home from shopping, and with her a friend.
Skirted and hosed, armed in swatches,
they burst into the dark room where Pilate

stands, watching Jesus lashed and crowned.
They lay swatches of plums and cherries
on the couch's back. Jesus' back runs
with blood. They turn, open the French doors

to the next room, and laugh. The cherries
will not do for the curtains. They look toward
the ceiling. My son looks at the cross.
It is heavy. He watches Christ stumble, fall.

I hear the tinkle of cups and voices. My wife
is happy. Christ dies slowly. The blood seeps
form his palms and his shoulders twist like
splayed ropes. The Roman soldier laughs,

hands him vinegar to drink. My wife drinks
coffee with her friend. No, she says, the cherries
are too bright. Christ lies wrapped in white.
His mother kisses him. My wife's friend rises

and kisses her. She is pleased that they have
shopped so well. The rock is rolled before
the tomb. My son lounges, legs draped, in silence.

# Carolyn's Poem

Easter was early that year and so was spring.
I have the pictures of the three, she in the
middle between the two boys, after church
on the steps, still in their new clothes,
full of blues and whites and the shoes you
could see your face in, and then later,
in the backyard the other picture in the
green chair of her holding the neighbor's
baby, with that look, you know, of loving.
It all came naturally to her. The thing
I tried to explain to the youngest later
was about that, how she had taught him too,
before she left, how to love. He still knows.
You see they had played together for two
years, sometimes for hours at a time
without us hearing them, and she knew
and imparted that gift, grace if you will.
And I keep thinking that when the spring
comes this time I will be over it and let
it come with that lightness of pink and
yellow but I can't unhook from the suddenness
of that leaving and the cherries and the
dogwoods. Maybe that is what I wanted to
tell you the day I didn't come. To tell you
that she has always been in the eyes of
the ones I have loved since. She would
have been eighteen in May. I pull back from
the young ones now. Out of fear for them
or me or both. I tell them nothing. But
you, if I didn't tell, it would be the sin
against the self. Let it rest at that.

# Out of Mourning

Spring again,
and I sit in the green chair reading.
The yellow dog noses among the neighbor's
daffodils. Over my book I watch for you
to come, waiting as I have all the nights
of my days for that moment beyond time
when April sorrows will be stilled by
the white flower in the moist red earth.

Did you know, my deep eyed dove, did you
know even then that August afternoon
as you danced in the willow's shade
that I who had been gone was standing
by the corner of the house watching
your whispered dreams?
                            Did you know
as you turned and looked and flowed
into my arms, locking your legs around
my waist, that you had hooked the very
marrow of my soul?
                        And did you know
that Easter morning as you cradled
the neighbor's child in your arms,
leaning your head against my knees
while I read in the April sun, that
the wind would blow over your grave
before another dawn?
                        Were these your gifts?
Waking or sleeping, I keep these images
inviolate, like mottled sunbeams through
winter windows or leaves long buried
in the beds of streams, kicked to the
surface by spring storms.

You grow
through the years. You are older
and the color in your cheeks runs
to red. Stand by my chair and put
your arms around my neck. Good.
I would feel that touch before another night.

# Before Forty

*"Why does it take men so long to grow up?"*
                    *—anonymous feminist*


I'll tell you why. My mother drank a lot.
One night she shot my father. They separated.
Tough it out, little man, with no parents.
Tears are for girls, said the cops with the
silver badges and the yellow stripes on the
blue sleeves. Then the phone ringing,
I don't know, maybe five years later,
and me, twelve, in the bed, curled tight,
and my nightgowned sister at the door.
Christ, I know what it is before she even
opens it. I ought to cry, I think, because
my mother's dead, but dead eyes don't make
tears, do they?
                    So we walk to the funeral
parlor in blue suits and dresses and me
dragged, silent, to look at a stranger
puffed up with rouge and lipstick and whatever
else they pour in the veins after the soul
flies. Then she was gone, and the sister
too, not dead, but swept, like Henry Fonda
and family in the *Grapes of Wrath*, kids in the
back seat reading Captain Marvel, boxes
tied with clothesline, husband at the wheel,
hair slicked down with Wildroot Cream Oil,
disappearing down the road to California.
Sweet Jesus, where was California, to a kid
nineteen years old who had to buy his own
bus ticket and didn't know how three thousand
miles could hurt. Tough it out, kid. You're
strong. Be a man.
74

Then, the daughter, too,
at thirty, as if the mother and the sister
weren't enough. To test him, maybe. Job.
Sitting in the church singing "O God Our
Help in Ages Past" and still dry eyed with
the rage helpless and blank and the room
upstairs suddenly empty and me walking the
steps in my sleep and coming home like Orpheus
empty handed.
          Come on, now, ladies, you do
like that? Then the crack up, the spinning
edgeward of the top on the kitchen table and
the Humpty Dumpty business of trying to make
a jewel of the cracked pieces of the heart.

So you want a happy ending? I don't know
much about that. I cry a lot these days.
Not for broken shoelaces or spilled beer,
but for Bach and the Beatles and for
beauty where I find it. I sleep later,
dream more, and write stuff like this.

Is it better?

# After

After the grass has been trimmed and
the beans picked, the flowers watered,
creeping plants plucked, and the dog
checked for fleas and ticks and other
crawling insects and the ants swept
from the kitchen floor into neat green
bags for disposal in the proper place

2

After the children have been marched
to the store for their fall clothing
and the drawers rearranged and the ten
year old cries in his brother's shirt
and the oldest flies to college, and the
youngest's behavior has been modified
by Montessori and the spouse sent packing
to the latest conference on conferences

3

After the course on small engine
repairs has been completed and the
automobiles, power motors, racing boats,
refrigerators, washing machines, dryers,
fans, and hair blowers have each been
meticulously disassembled, diagnosed
and surgically mended

After the United States Government has been
consulted and the pamphlets rigorously read
with special attention to italics and the
changes in tax law memorized and all the
proper forms duly filled out and notorized

After the Sunday *Times* has been read
in bed and crossword and jigsaw puzzles
pieced together and the Orange, Rose, Sugar,
Wintergreen, Spearmint, Tangerine, Wool, and
Lucite Bowls argued over, slept through,
and Saturday Night Live jived, and Archie
Bunker booed for the ninety-ninth time, and
*Playboy* plucked from the fourteen year old

After the face is made up, the collar tightened,
the tie tied, the girdle stretched, the dress
bought, the shoes shined, the stocking seamed,
the red coat returned for the beige, and
the luggage bought for the trip to France
and the smiles smiled, and the passports
paid for, and the Florida sun burns the
arms pink instead of brown

After the cousins are kissed and the grandparents
thanked and the old friends courted anew and
the tennis rackets resurrected once more for
the mayor's annual game and the tuxedo and
evening gown rented for the club ball and
the gold pen received for thirty years of
faithful service, and the hair rinsed to
take away the grey, and the teeth capped

After the sun has set, and the moon, and the
stars, and candles, and lanterns, and electric
lights, and fireflies, and the windows nailed
shut and the doors locked and the VACANT sign
placed in the yard, and the dogs lift their
legs in the long grass

Then I will . . . then you will . . . then we

Anthony S. Abbott was born in San Francisco. He was educated at Princeton and Harvard and is Charles A. Dana Professor of English Emeritus at Davidson College.

His poems have appeared in *New England Review, Southern Poetry Review, St. Andrews Review, Pembroke, Tar River Poetry*, and many others. *The Girl in the Yellow Raincoat* was first published by St. Andrews College Press in 1989 and was nominated for the Pulitzer Prize. He has two other poetry collections, *A Small Thing Like a Breath* and *The Search for Wonder in the Cradle of the World*.

He lives in Davidson, North Carolina with his wife Susan. They have three sons and six grandchildren.